CROW AND HERON

Jacques Moulin is a widely published and respected contemporary French poet, the author of many slim volumes, often produced in collaboration with visual artists. The varied coast line of his native Normandy often features in his work, as do the forests and rivers of the eastern region of France in which he now lives.

David Ball hails from Stoke-on-Trent, but now lives in retirement in France, where he reads, writes and translates. He has published four books in France, one of them a book of haiku in both English and French, *The Seasons in the Park/Les Saisons du parc*.

© 2025, Original text: Jacques Moulin, translation: David Ball. All rights reserved; no part of this book may be reproduced by any means without the publisher's permission.

ISBN: 978-1-917617-05-5

The author has asserted their right to be identified as the author of this Work in accordance with the Copyright, Designs and Patents Act 1988

Cover designed by Aaron Kent

Cover image: © Katrine_arty / Adobe Stock

Edited and Typeset by Aaron Kent

Broken Sleep Books Ltd
PO BOX 102
Llandysul
SA44 9BG

CONTENTS

CORBEAU / THE CROW	8
LE CORBEAU A QUELQUE CHOSE DES MUCOSITÉS DANS SON CRI / CROW HAS SOME SORT OF MUCUS IN HIS CALL	10
CORBEAU PARLE / CROW SPEAKS	12
LE CORBEAU EST UN CRI / THE CROW IS A CRY	14
FOI DE CHARBONNIER SANTÉ DE FER CORBEAU CROIX DE FER / BLIND BELIEF CROW'S IRON-HARD HEALTH HIS IRON CROSS	16
LE CORBEAU GARDE LA LUMIÈRE DANS SON NOIR / CROW MAINTAINS A LIGHT IN HIS DARKNESS	18
CORBEAUX EN GLANE DANS LES MAÏS LESSIVÉS / CROWS GLEANING IN THE WASHED CORN	20
TIENS VOILÀ DU HÉRON / SEE, THERE'S A HERON	22
BEC DANS LA BRÈME / BEAK IN THE FISH	24
TROIS HÉRONS AU PRÉ / THREE HERONS IN A FIELD	26
NOTES	31

For Marianne and Nicole

Crow and Heron

Jacques Moulin
Translated by David Ball

Broken Sleep Books

Corbeau
Encore haut
Pousse au noir
Son cri fort
Chaque soir
Proie du noir
Sous le ciel
Toujours haut
Du corbeau
Qui repasse
Tu rebrasses
Un corps lourd

The crow
keeping high up
raises each evening
to the dark
a raucous shout
A prey to the dark
under a sky
still high
crow
passing again
as you again take up
a heavy body.

Le corbeau a quelque chose des mucosités dans son cri

Le corbeau tousse une rauque couleur

Le corbeau coraille en luisant

Corbeaux en corvée par les champs tracas pour les croquants

Corvée de corbeaux pour rabattre aux champs n'effraie pas le croquant

Fourrage de corbeaux pour manger méchants est souvenir d'antan

Freux affairés jettent l'ancre à terre

Un freux bien lavé ne devient pas blanc

Soupe de freux n'est guère goûteuse

Crow has some sort of mucus in his call

crow coughs a hoarse colour

crow corals gleaming.

Hard at it over fields the crow's a problem for peasants

though their drives over the fields won't scare him off.

His fodder nasty mastication is in memory of old times.

Busy rooks anchor to the earth,

even well washed they don't whiten.

Rook soup is no tasty mouthful.

Corbeau parle
un pas beau dire
gras parler du corbeau
c'est pas peu dire
dit pas des mots
dit du cri
du cri croassant
du cri discordant
assez

Corbeau dit ni bruit ni cri
corbeau parle corbac
– crâ cré crou
croua crôa créa –
grosses grasses paroles
syllabiques et gutturales

Corbeau parle
ça lui vient du thorax
il y plonge le bec
enfle le cou baisse le chef
expectore

Corbeau parle
couramment
Corvus Corax

Crow speaks
not a pretty sound
a fat speech
it's not nothing
not words
it's the shout
the cry crowing
discordant
enough

Crow says no noise no cry
he speaks crowish
craa, cray, croo
crouah, croah, creah
big fat words
throaty syllables

When he speaks
it comes from the chest
he prods it with his beak
swells his neck lowers his head
spits

He speaks
fluent
Corvus Corax

Le corbeau est un cri
L'appel rauque du temps des genèses
Le corbeau est *l'oiseau de la première fois*

Il porte en lui l'homme
et la création

Le corbeau officie par trois fois
depuis sa fiente
– celle du vent des matières en fusion
et du fondement de l'être

Le corbeau chamane
– lumière en lui et voix des rêves

Le corbeau façonne
la courbure du monde
à l'aube primitive
quand râpe l'écorce de l'aulne

Le corbeau dans son cri
garde mémoire obscure

The crow is a cry
a hoarse call of first times
he's the bird of first time

He carries within him
man and the whole creation

as he officiates three times
from his droppings,
those blown from materials in fusion
or from the bottom of being

The crow a shaman:
the light within him and the dream voice

He shapes
the world's curve
to first dawn
alder bark grating

as he stores in his cry
some obscure memory

Foi de charbonnier santé de fer corbeau croix de fer. On ne comprend rien à ce qu'il rauque. Débite en copeaux ses cris qui brûlent le gosier râpent le cœur. Des cris grossiers. Le corbeau craille croasse mais croit-il dur comme fer à l'enfer qui l'attend ? Paroles de porteurs de sacs – toile de jute et charbon gras. De sorciers des suies.

Le corbeau fume sa vie aux juchoirs de villes noires qu'il étire en boulets jusqu'aux friches ou bien glane l'herbe grise des champs. Tous les champs sont filons des jours et griserie de gorge.

Blind belief crow's iron-hard health his iron cross. We understand nothing of his harsh voice. Spitting out shouts like woodchips which burn the throat, rasp the heart. Rough shouts. Crow craws and caws, but does he believe hard enough in the hell that awaits him? Trust the sack carriers – jute wrapped round bright black coal. Witchcraft of soot.

Crow smokes away his life on perches in black towns which he stretches out in heavy balls to waste ground or else gleans in grey grassy fields. Fields all of them seams of time and the throat's intoxication.

Le corbeau garde la lumière dans son noir
Le noir plumage dit la lumière intérieure du corbeau
Le corbeau a la forme noire des lumières retenues
Le corbeau s'irise au contact du couchant
À la nuit tombée le corbeau prend couleur de lune laiteuse
Le corbeau est blanc au profond de la nuit

Crow maintains a light in his darkness
his black plumage witness to his inner light
he has the black form of light held back
as he shines iridescent in the light of evening
night fallen he takes on a milky moon colour
in the depths of the night he's white

Corbeaux en glane dans les maïs
lessivés

Chaises en conversation vide
dans les vergers

La saison se rentre
feuilles écrasées

Blessures et rouilles
à terre

Infusion confusion

Tout file vers l'hiver
dans l'estime des bruyères

On reprendra corps avec le héron
cendré solitaire
qui patauge avant l'envol

On se dit qu'il y aura bien
quelque rose
et qui dure
pour la Noël

Crows gleaning in the washed corn

Chairs in empty conversation
in the orchards

The season folds in on itself
its leaves crushed

Wounds and rust reds
to ground

Infusion confusion

In the appreciation of heather
everything's on the move to winter

We'll recover form with the heron
ash-grey and solitary
paddling before take-off

We tell ourselves that there really will be
some sort of rose
one to last
for Christmas

Tiens voilà du héron
héron tourne en rond
autour du poisson

Bec dans l'eau
eau du bec glisse à l'eau

Tel va la route d'onde qu'à la fin elle se penche
sur sa commère l'eau
l'eau s'en revient à l'eau
ne s'épanche guère
héron non plus
toujours aux aguets
l'échauguette en dos

Juste un fil à couper
idée ou bien poisson

Faut quitter le piquet
puis plongeon

Au fond
héron tourne en rond

See, there's a heron
turning round
about a fish

Beak in the water
water sliding from beak to water

The way of the wave is such
that it leans over at last
its gossip the water
water returning to water
No opening out
the heron neither
always on the look out
a watch tower on his back

Just a thread to cut
an idea or better still a fish

Must come off the sentry post
then make a stab

At bottom he turns
round and round

Bec dans la brème
Comme un harpon
Héron glouton
Prend ce qu'il aime

Dès le jour blême
Est sur le pont
Bec dans la brème
Comme un harpon

Sans requiem
Pour le poisson
Stabat héron
Fait mi-carême
Bec dans la brème

Héron en S
Dans son corset
Refait le guet
Mais rien ne presse

Son œil ne cesse
De naviguer
Héron en S
Dans son corset

Quand il se baisse
C'est pour pêcher
Son déjeuner
Pas de prouesse
Héron en S

Three herons in a field
waiting for night
the road noisy
the traffic busy

Three ash-grey herons
or just simply grey
in a field
waiting for night

Night risen
would they fancy
frolicking
in the cut hay
the three herons?

Two herons in a field
one walking like an ostrich
the other a log
upright as a post

It will soon be summer
you can take off your hood
Two herons in the field
one walking like an ostrich

The first a wader
a touch feminine
strips with his beak
each blade of cut grass
the two herons in a field

Un héron au pré
Ne craint plus la buse
Qui là-haut s'amuse
À voler planer

Il a son carré
Au bord de l'écluse
Un héron au pré
Ne craint plus la buse

Les bateaux montés
Armada confuse
Si je ne m'abuse
Ont l'oiseau chassé
Héron loin du pré

One heron in a field
has no fear of the buzzard
amusing itself
floating high up

He has his spot
at the edge of the lock
no fear of the buzzard
this heron in the field

The boats come up
a mixed armada
have if I'm not mistaken
scared off the bird
the heron far from the field

NOTES

The first six poems are taken from the collection *Corbeline* (2022), the remaining four from À vol *d'oiseaux* (2013), both published by L'Atelier contemporain.

EXPOSE TON MALAISE

www.ingramcontent.com/pod-product-compliance
Lightning Source LLC
LaVergne TN
LVHW041313080426
835510LV00009B/968